What is adoption?

What is adoption

Sometimes families just can't live together, so it is necessary to find another family who will love and take care of the children.

Becoming part of a new family is called adoption.
Here are some reasons why families can't live together...

Some people are just too young to be parents.
They have no experience to raise a child.

Some parents want to keep their babies, but their families don't support them.

Some moms have a baby, but there's no dad or mom to help her and she feels that she can't raise the baby because it's really hard to do it all by yourself!

Sometimes a social worker or judge decides it would be best for a child to be adopted because some parents may have...

A serious problem with drugs or alcohol.

Some parents may have physically hurt or were not kind to their children and they just didn't know how to parent anyone! And they need some parent training!

Some may have gotten scared and moved away.
Leaving the baby all alone.

Some parents are unable to provide food, clothing, and even a safe place to live.

Some parents may have died.

Some parents may be incarcerated or in jail for breaking the law.

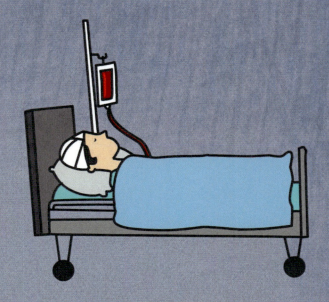

Some may have had a physical or mental illness and need hospitalization. It's not that they don't want to parent, they just can't parent like a child needs.

Most times, there's a team of people working to help keep the birth family together.

Social workers are helpers for parents and are also there to help the children feel safe and cared for. They will try to help and solve problems by creating a family "case plan."

Sometimes the plan calls for a child to live in foster care with foster parents, while their first parents work on the problems with the social worker. But if the problems can't be fixed, an adoption plan is made.

"An adoption plan" is made by the birth family and a social worker, who collectively decide it is the best thing for the health of the child. A judge then helps to finalize the adoption plan, and provides a permanent home for the child.

So you see, a social worker is a very important person in adoption because they help to find a family that is best for the child.

Social workers are there to be kind and supportive!

Even still, sometimes finding a family can take a long time and that's why some kids wait in a foster home, a group home, or with a relative for a while.

Until the parents, social worker, and the judge can figure things out.

The bottom line is children need love! When you are adopted, it means you have a new family, a new relationship as a daughter, a son, a sister or a brother, and you have become a very important part of your new family.

Its' important because you will be sharing all of life's experiences together. Birthdays, holidays, vacations, and so much more!

You will have many questions about your birth family, and you have every right to wonder and know the story of your adoption.

Ask your parents by making a question box
of questions and see what answers you can find?

...and what answers you can hold onto in your questions box.

Which brings along sad and mad feelings. All of these feelings are normal, because you are grieving the loss of your first family. This is called grief. You will need to grieve in order to feel better.

There is no right, there is no wrong. Expressing your feelings, can sometimes be hard. But the more you can do it, the better off you'll be.

Big Feelings will come and big feelings will go, like a great big wave so just go with the flow, don't push them away, make them your friend, so you can understand your grief and go play again!

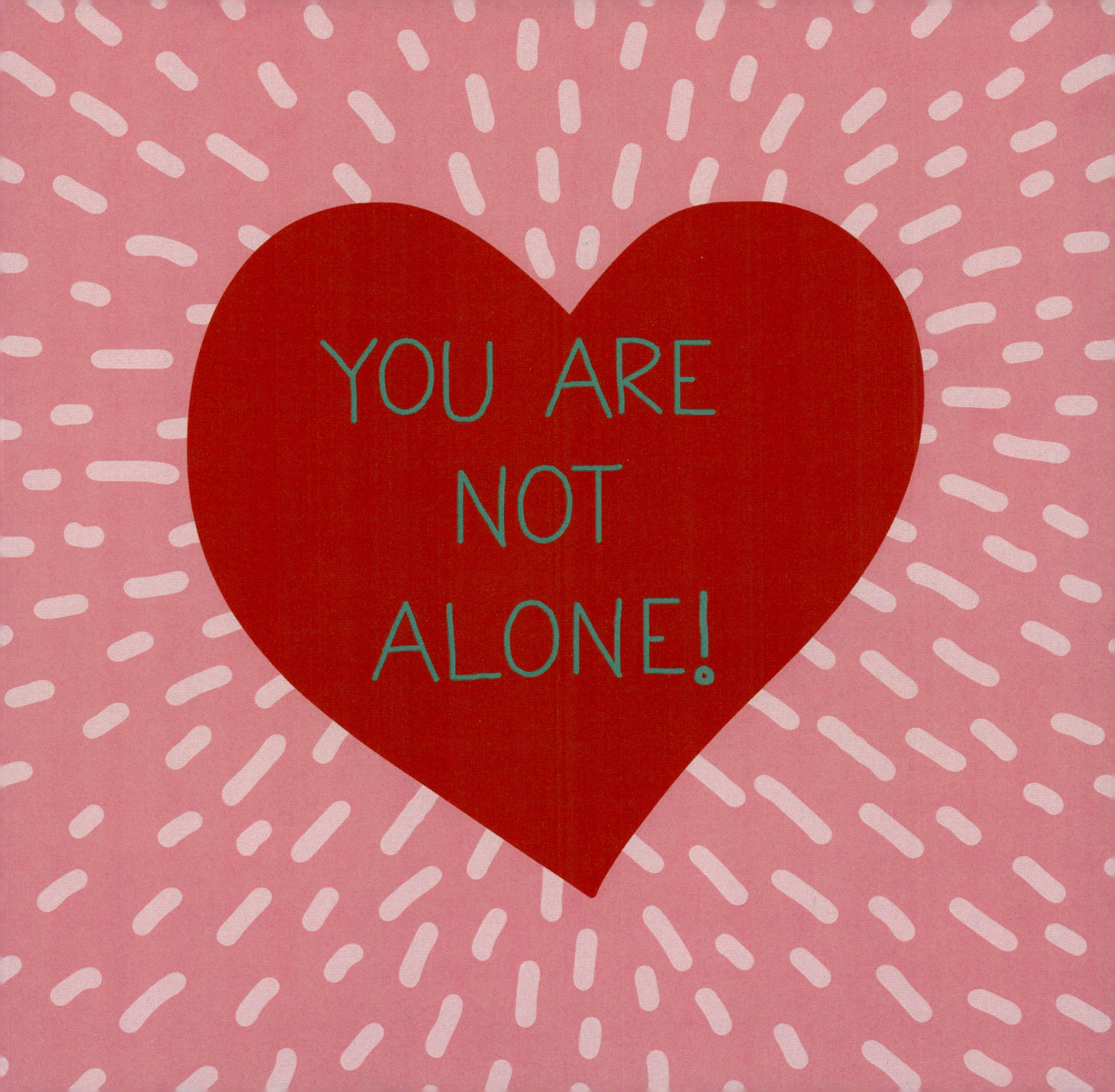
YOU ARE
NOT
ALONE!

But one thing to remember you are not alone!
There are 1.5 million children currently adopted
in the United States.

Between 1-2 million couples want to adopt a child 40 percent of adopted children are of a different race, culture, or ethnicity than both of their adoptive parents and 6 out of 10 Americans have a personal connection to adoption.

All of these people were adopted too!!! Colin Kaepernick, Faith Hill, Jamie Fox, Run DMC Daryl McDaniel's, Dave Thomas — Wendy's Founder, Steve Jobs, Marilyn Monroe, Simone Biles, Sarah McLachlan, Kristen Chenowith, Ray Liotta, Blondie, Keisha Cole, Liz Phair and many, many more.

Each year there are 135,000 children adopted in the United States. AND OVERALL, there are 7 million people adopted in the United States!!!

You are not alone

Jeanette Yoffe has been providing therapy, support, and education to children, teens, adults and their families connected by foster care and adoption since 1999. She is an author, speaker, and psychotherapist in Los Angeles.

Her passion comes from her own experience of being adopted at age 7 1/2, and raised in foster care for 6 years. She wrote a play about her experience, which can be found on Audible titled, *"What's Your Name, Who's Your Daddy?"*

Originally from New York, she lives in Los Angeles with her husband and son. She also has adopted 5 cats!!

Visit: www.JeanetteYoffe.com

Devika Joglekar is an animator and illustrator. She has provided illustrations for more than 50 children's books and over a dozen graphic novels, poetry books, comics. She has extensive experience creating art through various mediums like watercolor, ink, pencil, and photoshop.

She has been bringing ideas to life through her labor of love, *miheika.com.*

Originally from India, she now lives with her husband in San Francisco Bay Area.